Mind Full of Mad Verse

LIZ BENTLEY

CHIPMUNKA CLASSICS

CHIPMUNKA CLASSICS

All rights reserved, no part of this publication may be reproduced by any means, electronic, mechanical photocopying, documentary, film or in any other format without prior written permission of the publisher.

Published by
Chipmunkapublishing
United Kingdom

http://www. chipmunkaclassics.co.uk

Copyright © Liz Bentley 2015

ISBN   978-1-78382-211-9

Hello
I'm Liz Bentley

I am a poet, writer, comedian, musician, performer, raconteur, BACP senior accredited psychotherapist, clinical supervisor, group facilitator, lecturer, mother, step mother, partner, ex-partner, friend, facebooker, nudist, sun worshipper, follower of Multiple Sclerosis Recovery Diet, wine lover and I'm a sex and diary fanatic (I like a new diary 9 months before the year is out).
Currently I work at Goldsmiths and Lewisham colleges and have a private supervision practice. I perform regularly aiming to close the gap between comedy, mental health and disability. Over the years I have performed with Ruby Wax, Will Self, Susie Orbach, Liz Carr, Mat Fraser, John Hegley, Josie Long, Dolly Sen among many others and I got drunk with my childhood idol David Soul (also performing poetry) at the Samuel Beckett Happy Days festival in Enniskillen. I have performed at London Literary Festival (Southbank), National Theatre, Ledbury Poetry Festival, Dada Fest, Freud Museum among many other venues, festivals, conferences and training days, also in five swimming pools (including Liz Bentley-on-Sea, Edinburgh Fringe) and in a beach hut. I see my hairdresser every six weeks, my homeopath every two months and my yogic Thai masseur every four weeks. I practice Bikram and other yoga 3xweekly and I see a Tesco delivery man twice a week. I have a Master's degree on the subject of Psychotherapy and Psychosomatics.

Previous info: www.lizbentley.co.uk
Bookings: msliz.bentley@btinternet.com

Goodbye
Liz Bentley

Cuts

Cuts are a common type of injury
They can be treated easily
At home
You don't even have to phone
NHS direct

Apartheid at Resuscitation Training

The doctors are black and one Asian who sits ajar

The white receptionists sit at the head of the room

The nurses are black and they are late, they sit opposite the doctors

I, the therapist, sit in between the black doctors, opposite the Asian doctor, diagonal to the black nurses and adjacent to the reception staff and one white medical secretary

We do this once every 2 years. Nothing changes apart from the number of compressions, 20, 30, 40, then back to 20 again, etc, and the quality and chemical smell of the wet wipes gets worse and the dummies get grubbier

Ray, our trainer, asks if we have any questions. I want to go home

Just when we have completed our feedback forms one of the doctors asks whether we need to check if a child is pubescent so we know whether to perform child or adult resuscitation

Ray looks, pauses and says "perhaps that's not necessary"

One of the reception staff argues that the person could be a midget, so checking would prove necessary

I say "In our current climate I would rather be sued by a small person than find myself on a paedophile register"

The Lilo of Double Standards Part 1

My first boyfriend slept on a double air bed
He kept finches we loved and let out but found them dead
After one night of passion and rolling around
He didn't tell me until years later that he had found
The crushed little bodies, soft but ground
Into the grooves of the inflatable lilo of double standards

At 23 I joined the Samaritan volunteers
I was very good at it, got on well with my peers
I was more suicidal than the callers
I could be big, they could be smaller
It gave me purpose and made me think
It was seven years later I ended with my shrink
Travelled the world and floated in the pools
On the lilo of double standards

A Dublin man I met and wanted to marry
He worked, I loved him, but his parents were wary
In order to wed we fled to Fiji
He bailed out on New Year Eve
I wasn't that naïve
I had a grass skirt made for me
I wiggled my hips and played the ukulele
And swam on the lilo of double standards

The Lilo of Double Standards Part 2

I had a holiday booked when my mother was dying
She had days to live, it was just over a week I was due flying
I rang the funeral directors but they were unable to book
She had to be dead first, but they did have a look
At the diary where a bank holiday appeared
My mother had to die that day
Or I would not get to go away

The thunderstorm stopped her heart
Crematorium - Terminal - her depart
Gatwick – North Terminal - my depart

Twenty four hours it took to book
My dad with Alzheimer's got out his cheque book
My sister was pleased, she had to get back to Wales
To her husband working on the farm
Before he did any self-harm
The funeral went quick and well
I necked back the whiskey and danced 'til the last bell
The next day I stepped into the Aegean Sea
And grieved on the lilo of double standards

Security Man

(Man with poor communication skills and projection that it's the woman who is the insecure needy one)

I did my best and tried not to show my insecurities while my boyfriend was away staying with our old drama tutor whom he had previously enjoyed a homosexual relationship with

I didn't text him once, nor did he receive any missed calls from me

On returning he said

"I missed you"

"What did you miss about me?" I asked

"I missed you missing me"

Paul the Ocado delivery man in the courgette van (no missing items) did it for me

I decided it was still too soon to ask my new boyfriend to turn my mattress

Aversion Therapy for my 12 year old boy

The devil reincarnated
Play Station Three
More evil than a wee
Beware the devil console
With evil on its mind
Beware the devil console
It's gonna get you eating pizza with very large thumbs
Stop now. Stop now. We had a deal
Your deal. Stop now. No. Now
That's it. Don't call me an idiot. Or a loser. You little fucking shit. Sit down here.
No watch it, watch it, that's it, watch it
Angry German boy on PS3, YouTube, that's it watch him. Watch how fat he is, he's got no friends… look, he's got no console now, he's smashed it up, all that's left is an empty pizza box
Good, right, let's have a game of cards and a sing song around the piano

Separation from my 6 year old girl

Did you miss me Daisy?
I missed Donna Summer in the car
Did daddy tell you she'd died?
Yes, but we can still listen to her songs

Too late to have a shower

MS attack, boyfriend's back, in the sack, spunk on back
Massage therapist arrives, spunk dried

My First Cigarette

The Great War for Civilization

A bullet ricochets off the tobacco tin covering his heart, into his shoulder

Saves his life – cliché but true

I am 9 years old and the corner shop won't sell me fags and the machines are empty of ten Sovereign filter, No 6 and Piccadilly with the sixpence sellotaped on the packet

I take out one of the pre-rolled cigarettes from the 1914 Ligget and Myers tobacco tin

Parched, it burns up quickly

A bit falls off and leaves a hole in my brownie uniform

Adele Stanton comes round for tea and we smoke one together

Kevin Bottomley from round the back has another

Forty years later there are 6 pre rolled cigarettes left in the Liggett and Myers tobacco tin

I am not giving this to the Imperial War museum as suggested. They are there if I need one

Shagging With Freud

Freud would shag me in exactly the right way
He would always know when to come and when to stay
The boundaries would be clear but inside those fantasies would steer
Into the most passionate wet experience
No love, no mother, no father
Just
No anxiety

Gritty
Pretty
Shitty
And, just no anxiety

NB: There would of course be a line of coke in there somewhere

Ken Dodd's Dad's Dog's Dead

Where's the dog?
The dog's dead
Where's the dog?
The dog's dead
Where's the dog?
The dog is dead

Oh yes, he was doing piddles on the kitchen floor
No dad he collapsed and couldn't get up anymore

Where's your mother?
My mother's dead
Where's your mother?
My mother's dead
Where's your mother?
My mother's dead

Oh yes, she's next door making sure their cat is fed
No dad she died in a hospital bed

Ken Dodd's Dad's dog's dead

The Dying Song

I'm dying, you're dying, we're all dying of different things
I'm dying, you're dying, we're all dying of different things

Will I be at your funeral or will you be at mine?
Will I be at your funeral or will you be at mine?

It's just a matter of time

I'm dying, you're dying, we're all dying of different things
I'm dying, you're dying, we're all dying of different things

Will I be at your funeral or will you be at mine?
Will I be at your funeral or will you be at mine?
It's just a matter of time

The older generation are dropping like flies
We're the next ones who are going to die
Do you believe in life after death?
When will you take your very last breath?

Peri menopause song

You're hot baby
You're really hot baby
You're really, really hot, baby
"It's you that makes me hot, baby"

Origami

Origa me

Out of newspaper

The Saturday Guardian please

I am size 8 on top and age 12/13 years bottom

Size 4 feet, but if you are making me with my motorbike gear on then you better make that size 5 – room for thick socks in the winter

I would like the travel section as my intestine

The TV guide as my arse, and the financial pages up my arse

And my head, I would like all other words to be cut up into letters that spell as many times as is possible

'Fuck the big society'

Great fuck

Heating on
Heating off
Door open
Door closed
Forward Planning
See what happens
Open house
Empty house
Feeling
Thinking
Upset
Anger
Anger
Rage
Eastenders
Star Trek
Great fuck

Sickness
Health
Sickness
Psychosomatic symptoms
Sickness
Bad Back
Nurse
Child
Mother
Child
Child
Narcissism
Talking

Listening

Talking

Hand over mouth

Shouting

Retreat to cave

Talking

Accusation of nagging

Talking

Door slamming

Screaming

Retreat to Cave that is located further away

Screaming (possibly hysterical symptoms if we are to think about hysteria in modern society as opposed to Freud's original thinking)

Cave door locked

Stressed

Depressed

Crying

Silence

Sobbing

Silence

Calls friends

Silence

Eastenders

Star Trek

Great fuck

The Twin Room (I had planned to buy some Cromer crabs before I came home but it didn't quite work out that way)

Cromer family holidays, all their lives, some of our lives

Mother's ashes off the pier

Dad having a beer – in the Red Lion

Virginia Court hotel - 2 nights – with Paul and Sue, Paul is Gina's son, Gina had an affair with my dad for years, Paul and Sue don't know this, they are older than me and my sister and I had already left home

We love our dad, they love our dad, he looked after their mum in more ways than one. She's dead now

My sister's friend's mum died suddenly the week before Cromer, so night number 2, she has to leave for a funeral and I'm on my own

Dad pisses himself, can't find the ensuite, locks himself out of the room

The hotel mislead us, we asked if there was 24 hour service if we had any problems, they said no, however, in the morning, they said someone would have got up, like fuck

Dad takes his wet pyjama bottoms off and sleeps in the twin bed, next to me

Getting up every hour to pee – like an unsettled newborn I'm neglecting, I'm fucked off, I'm not sleeping, "I told you the toilet is there" I say x 8.

My childhood, when he had Gina, but couldn't have her, he had the twin bed in my room

How did my mother not see that this was not good for me?

Lying next to me – wanking

Like a tap dripping leaving stains on adolescent porcelain

Drip

Drip

Drip

When morning came the chef gave me the master key, I took dad back to his room, made him a cup of tea

Then I left, leaving dad with Paul and Sue, bewildered

Of course, I would never tell them anything

I want them to have him again at Xmas

Dropping the Kids Off

Rare for me to hang out at the school gates
But my 5 year old was giving out her party invites
The 1st received was going away
The 2nd just looked away

Then they came

THE CONTROLLING MOTHERS

Of course I wasn't to know
Wednesday's child, full of woe in the same class
Had her party on that very same afternoon
She's full of woe because her mother is so fucking miserable

The controlling mothers came nearer, and nearer
In defence, some have carried guns, others run
Unprepared and school gates now closed
I put my hands up in the air

"You will have your party in the morning" the biggest one said
"Two hours is long enough" the middle one said
"But I have a fairy coming from Coventry, she's already bought her train ticket, she won't get there on time" I said
"You can be the fairy" the smallest one said
"Ok, I'll be the fucking fairy" I screamed
I didn't return to the school that day. It was their dad's turn to pick them up
They probably thought I was scared
I was

I'm Happy

I'm happy, I'm happy

I'm happy, I'm happy

I'm not happy anymore

Smack my bum, I've got a lump sum

I am a pensioner
I am a pensioner

I started getting my pension in March
It's taxed and I didn't know that

I am a pensioner
I am a pensioner

It may seem unreal
But I had to appeal
Was sent to see a psychiatrist
To check I wasn't just depressed
One of the best things about being a medically retired pensioner with an NHS pension
Is that I'm never allowed to work in the NHS ever again
So if I'm on the iPad
And see an ad
I'm not sad
It's fab

I'm a pensioner
I'm a pensioner
At 49
I can draw a line
Start on my bucket list
And Google cruise lines

Freudian Slip

His mother wanted no other intimate relationship

Than that with her son

Exclusivity

She bought a house

His bedroom had no door and the door to the only bathroom was the door in his room

His door was the door to her room

His father wanted inclusivity

The boy had already learned and cried for his exclusivity

His mother, delighted, under a guise of, he is a bad father, men are bad

His father, not the 'fathers for justice' kind of a guy accepted them as a couple

They are a couple

At 8 he made an attempt to separate

He joined a football club

His mother, hating football, became the club manager

She used to be a keen swimmer. I asked her why she didn't swim anymore

I stopped when I met him, she said, then corrected herself and said

I stopped when I had him

He kicks a ball, she blows the whistle

Halloween

I was driving through the Rotherhithe Tunnel
I turned off the windscreen wipers
Then had to turn them back on

Drs Appointment

I woke up in the middle of the night, 3.08 am
I noticed patches of my skin had turned yellow
I put two and two together

I rang my family and friends
To tell them of my fate
It could only be liver sclerosis
And I'd probably left it too late
All those years of alcohol consumption
I hadn't got away with past self-destruction

At 8.30am I was knocking at the Dr's door
At 9am the doctor was on the computer to check out more
About my assumption
Silence
Then, "Ah, it's about your carrot consumption"
"Carrotina is what it's called. You have a carrot addiction"
I cried that I had not died, before my time, but
What are the harmful consequences of a carrot addiction?
Health, personal development opportunities
Divorce, loss of standing in communities
Self image, self image, self image
Time wasted, financial consequences, press exposure,
Encouraging other addictions such as peppers, courgettes, organic ladies' fingers
Living in fear of being found out.
Living in fear of being found out

Back at home a friend had arrived to help me in my distress
She took me up to bed, to calm me down, catch up on sleep
Then she noticed on my dress – ing table
The moisturizer I had been using was tinted

We laughed and when my friend had gone
I picked up the bottle of moisturizer
Its ingredients alarmed me

Golden Balls

You came to my aid during my MS attack
Cooked for me to keep me on track
With my recovery
And as we see
It's going according to plan

But I want to know what you make of this
A colleague at work knew I was unfit
And lent me the DVD of Golden Balls

I watched it with Graeme our once number one fan
Who came to see Rolf at the Old Bailey with me and you Caroline Anne
Through the abusive relationships, threesomes and such
For the main character it got too much
In a wheel chair he ends up

Of course the prostitute in the film also has a sticky end
She dies in a car crash, now let's not pretend
It was last week we spoke about possible prostitution
I'd met Janice at the Sun rooms and with her a constitution
We talked of the pros and the cons and
How she had to adapt to the request for strap-ons
She couldn't formulate an outside relationship well
But for 4 weeks a year she did dwell
With her 30 year old Egyptian lover

Start late she advised, she started at 50 and gave up at 59

But had had a great time

And more importantly had earned loads and loads of dosh

But her daughter-in-law dobbed her in to her son

"Mother, you're a whore" he said, not keen on prostitution

Anyway Caroline Anne,

I'd like you to watch Golden Balls

And see what you think

And please if you can tell me the link

Why a colleague gave it to me to watch?

I'm itching and scratching and itching and scratching to understand why

All I know is that someone fell in love with him and 2 weeks ago of suicide she did die

Poor Old/Young Justin Bieber

I took my 7 year old daughter to the 02 arena on 3rd March 2013

You may be thinking, but Justin Bieber didn't start his 3 nights at the 02 until 4th March

You would be right in thinking this, nor was Justin Timberlake anywhere near the arena on this date

It was Girls Aloud we were at the 02 to see.

I was dying to tell someone what a great occasion this would be

But I didn't think anyone would understand

Justin having been exceedingly late for his show on 4th March, resulting in weeping girls being taken home on the last train by irate mothers

No Justin for them that night, poor little mites

This bad show from Mr Bieber has helped me express, less ashamedly, my passion for the girls, particularly Nicola who is writing a lot of their new songs and Sarah who is looking good after rehab. I am not commenting on Cheryl's new tattoo, but if she saw mine she may regret as they fade and don't look so nice 30 years later and it's really painful getting them off

The girls were on stage prompt at 8.35pm. They sang 19 hits and after being showered with red and white feathers, we left the arena and were both tucked up in bed by 11pm

Tower Blocks

I always wanted to live in a tower block
As a child I envied Mary, Mungo and Midge

25 years ago I moved in with Kevin, a beautiful Scottish carpenter whose beauty deteriorated as his heroin addiction was built upon. His flat was on the 15th floor of a tower block in Green Dragon Lane, right by Kew Bridge station. Those ones near the London Museum of Water and Steam, easily seen from the A4 going onto the M4.

Jokingly, Kevin picked me up one day and dangled me out of the 15th floor tower block we lived in.

My new man lives on the 8th floor. He is moving in with me in November. He is also a carpenter

I dreamt last night that my new boyfriend's brother moved in with him and I had to have sex with his brother while he watched over. I told him my dream in the morning. He reassured me and told me that his brother would only pass by occasionally for a cup of tea.

Oats

Oats and sex
Oats equals sex
Everything equals sex
Everything is a penis or a vagina
Container or a stork

At work I complained about how computers were taking over my job
The doctors suggested I needed more mouse control
My neighbours and I decided enough was enough and we needed mouse control
A pest control man came 4 times
On the 4th visit he told me he liked my hair
On this occasion I took him up upstairs to block the holes in my ensuite
With that wire stuff
He told me his 2 boys had chicken pox
I told him that when my kids had chicken pox I bathed them with porridge oats in a muslin cloth which was very soothing

Child diagnosis

"Everyone in my class knows that Anya's from Greece apart from Qudos," said Daisy age 9

"Why's that," I asked

"He's artistic" she replied

I went to see the Damned at the Roundhouse on Saturday

I went to see the Damned at the Roundhouse on Saturday
I walked in the outside bit where other Damned fans were smoking
Drunk I hollered "Has anyone got any drugs today?"
Heads turned away
But one gentleman said "It's been a long time since anyone asked me that"
In the mosh I screamed for 'Disco Man'
No drugs but from the bar I stole a very small but special pork pie worth £2.50

Michael Jackson's Support

Michael Jackson was 50 years old when he died
I'm 50, 25th June 1914, if I survive
25th June was when his doctor tried to keep him alive
Unlawfully so
He wasn't to know
Was anyone supporting the doctor?

After this show
I go home alone (my 101th boyfriend not here tonight)
I used to have giardia a parasite
I was never alone at night
A comforting thought in my mind as I lay
Even though giardia was eating me away

My lodger moved out today
My 101th boyfriend will be moving in soon, to stay
He's painting our room
Keeping the windows open
So I don't breathe in the fumes
He can't however stop me to die
From any excessive wine
That's up to me, my responsibility
But I had my liver checked out recently
All was ok
But not for DLT
And what about Jim Davidson on CBB?
This day 8 years ago Rula Lenska was being evicted from the house
I was pulling my placenta out

In a pool in the front room
I didn't eat it though
Just had a little look
To see if the wine had got through a nook
All is well
Of course I'll go to hell
Will be lots of fun
Not dissimilar from my addiction for Bikram torture yoga and lying in boiling sun
Bikram Choudhury, may be a sex pest, is due in court soon

Feeling deflated and let down

My friend said that she's never had a problem with air beds
I feel like a whole chapter of my life has been spent buying and blowing

The Country Mouth and the Town Mouth

We put our lipstick on before the log man and the Tesco delivery man arrive

The log man doesn't come as frequently as the Tesco delivery man

The log man has fingers missing and shows his strength and bottom

The Tesco delivery man comes frequently and is usually a different man each time

He shows minimal strength and not his bottom

The shed is full of wood
The fridge is full of food
As we lick our lipstick away

Hello. How are you?

I'm really busy
I'm busy
I'm so busy
I'm soooo busy
I'm very busy
I'm so very busy
I'm soooooooooooo busy
I'm soooooooooooo very busy
Busy man
So busy
Sooooooooooo busy
Man, so busy
Man, man, sooooooooo busy
Woh, really really busy mate
Phrrrrrrrrr. Just busy

Goodbye

Faster Catheter Kill Kill

(nb Twoc is short for Trial Without Catheter)

Dick twoc
Dick twoc
Dick twoc

Trickery dickery twoc
Authorised by the doc
The clock struck one
The device is on
Trickery dickery twoc

Trickery dickery twoc
A tube instead of a cock
The clock strikes three
The patient wees
Trickery dickery twoc

Trickery dickery twoc
The infection ran up to the clock
The clock strikes five
The patient dies
Trickery dickery twoc

Dick twoc
Dick twoc
Dick twoc
Dick twoc

Stubble Reverse on Bookface

London Bridge Bikram hot yoga Studio Monday 12th January 2015

"I'm the king of the jungle" is piped through speakers in reception

"It's ginger day," said one of the staff who was wearing a beanie hat but clearly ginger underneath

"This means that anyone can kiss me today"

"Oh," I said "Is there a kiss a menopausal, short woman with multiple sclerosis day?"

I persevered with jealous feelings which were enhanced on sight of a ginger person in the yoga class

Out of class and in the shower it was hard to work out if there were any other gingers there that day

Most women dye their hair and my research suggests that most women under the age of 30 (and most women who attend hot Bikram yoga classes are under 30) have Hollywood vagina waxing

I used to think this was linked to self-harm or porn but more recently it has become quite obvious that the hair removed from the young women is now on young men's faces. I realized this well before I saw the pictures of the transformation of hair from women's vaginas to men's faces on Facebook. I had made this connection a long time before this. Often ahead of my time but not in the omnipotent/omniscient sort of a way

Morbid Jealousy and Mindfulness

The first night I stayed at my 100th boyfriend's abode
We went to his bedroom for us to unload
Frustrated feelings from time gone past
I came first he came last

In the morning he got up and left the bedroom
I wondered where he'd gone, it felt too soon
When he came back I asked him "What was the time?"
He'd been gone for one minute and 39
Seconds, I asked him "Where have you been?"
He said "to the bathroom to make my teeth gleam"
Had I not breathed, it would have been difficult that day
To use the bathroom in a normal way
It's not unusual to be jealous of a room
If I hadn't breathed, it could have ended in doom
I think
I might have been sick in the sink

Get to the Point

BBC radio London
Vanessa Feltz was giving away a free bottle of champagne
To whoever came up with the best story
Of drinking champagne in an unusual way

First I told her producer of my tale of woe
Where in Fiji I was rejected by my bow
Hotel management had left the bottle in the room
To lighten the load as my spinster days did loom

But when eventually Vanessa picked up the phone
She asked how I was and I told her I was alone
She thought that that was my story of drinking champagne
And put the phone down

Another caller won that bottle
I was gutted and have never rung Vanessa since
I wince
Every time she comes on the radio
I'm really pissed off still after all these years because I should have won that bottle as the person who won didn't have a good story at all and Vanessa shouldn't have cut me off before I told her the story which was much more interesting than the other callers. Still now she thinks I rang to win a bottle of champagne with a story of just being alone. I think I'm going to clear the air and email her right now, get straight to the point and maybe she will be able to revert back to how it felt when she was on Celebrity Big Brother and have some empathy for me and get me the free bottle of champagne that I think I rightly deserve. After all, her producer was really keen on my story and if she asks

her producer they will remember my story as they thought it very funny.

Hospital Food

A nice man from the ward domestic staff team gave me
a tray of food
"That looks nice" I said
"Believe me, it's horrible" he said

Motability cuts

My neighbour was so jealous of my Motability BMW convertible
She said she was going to cut off her leg
Sadly the envy ate her away from the inside out
A car was no longer necessary to her requirements

The People's NHS

For me, things started to change in 2006
I was required to ignore free association and dreams
Focus on CBT
Cognitive Behavioural Therapy
Cock and Ball Torture and reams
Of paperwork

Change your thoughts
Don't believe
Become a Stepford wife
Leave the webs to weave
Unwoven for another life

I arrived one day at my office to find that my new computer was bigger than my therapy chair
From that day I learned more about our computer man's relationships
Than that of my own patients

I checked my emails
'Benefits advisor, cut, Dietitian, cut'
Then a knock at the door
Three nice young men in overalls
"We have come to measure your radiator" they chimed
It was the end of the tax year
Health and safety pockets lined
The excuse, someone had died
Falling out of bed onto a radiator

Once the radiator cover was built and installed into my counsellor's shrine
(and into every consulting room, not just mine)

I noticed the nice men had omitted to cut a hole where I would be able to change the temperature

It took time to get the key to unlock the cover of the radiator

To take it off

Every time it was hot

Or cold or cold or hot

That key and cover were so stiff

I needed my computer man to shift

To turn it up or down

Down or up

Then .....

The forms came marching 2 by 2 hoorah, hoorah

The forms came marching 4 by 4 hoorah, hoorah

The forms came marching 6 by 6

There's only time for a temporary fix

And they all went marching, down to the arc to get out of the cuts boom, boom, boom

The ship of relations became an arc of robotics

Clinical supervision was questioned and funds taken away

Management supervision now, more forms and box ticking

Volunteers gone, no funds to support them

And as my support was taken from me

It was easy to see

Why my MS kicked in

I had to use my walking stick to get myself in

To work

Or not to work?

That was the question

And as for the patients
My needs took over theirs
And the new psychologists weren't aware
It's not their fault
They are required to vault
From box to box
Helpless to helpless
With nowhere to refer
The arc almost sank
Thank God for the food bank
And suicide note
That keeps the helpers afloat

And you need to vote
And protest
Before you are bereft
Of the NHS

Ode to my psychoanalytical psychotherapist

1 year 1 x weekly
2 years 3 x weekly
4 years 4 x weekly
Total: 1012 sessions
On her couch
South, of the river
In one of those council flats facing Saint Paul's
Which are now ex-Council flats

She kept me alive for 7 years
On very reduced fee
30 years on she sent me
A cheque for £1,000
A yoga retreat I found
Practising inside and out

Barbara has had a stroke
Like my mother who is dead
But the mother inside my head
Is dying

My carpenter is back from the workshop

Today I got my spirit level
With my sliding bevel
I screwed in with the impact driver
Today the random orbital sander
Came in handier
Than the scraper
And the stud detector wasn't sure
Whether to use the circular or the Japanese saw

My cordless drill, will with the offset chuck
And the moisture meter will tell me
If you are ready to fuck
Tonight

Whether you wear the PVA or the PU glue
With my forstner bit I will screw driver you
We can have a bit of fun
With the pincers, mole grips and the
 No nonsense foam applicator gun

And if the sash or G-clamp gets too much
I'll use the Vernier gauge and edge with the edge bander
¼ or ½ inch router
And belt sander

Now it's time for a biscuit
Joiner and count my chisels

Tomorrow I'll get onto the wood turning lathe
And mortisser (which is not set up yet)

And have a go with the bastard file
Though this is crossing a line
And verging on metal work

It's time for bed
With my long nose plyers
Quick check in the mirror
At the pillar, drill
And reciprocating saw
And laminate trimmer

Dental floss is absolutely fantastic

Thanks to being bulimic for most of my teens
My gums became rotten and my teeth did not gleam
But when I realized what a terrible mess
I was in, and not looking my best
I stopped throwing up
And went to the doc
Who sorted me out
And I flossed every day
Up, down and every way
Then the bleeding stopped
I could open my chops
With a beautiful smile
And the teeth whitener lasts a while

Claim to Fame

I was hairy corn-flaked at a radio roadshow in Great Yarmouth

MSC Cruise

A cruise
The food
Institutionalised within a day
Didn't get off the ship
All week
To pay
Any attention to anything
But the ocean

"All hands aboard boy, All hands aboard boys
The ship is calling for more.
We're getting ready, now for a steady
To pull away from the home shore
We're off to find adventure any how
Because we know that now

We're riding along on the crest of a wave and the sun is in the sky
All of our eyes on the distance horizon look out for passers by
We'll do the hailing, when all the ships around are sailing
We're riding along on a crest of a wave and the world is ours!"

That's Ralph Reader, Gang Show writer extraordinaire but he's dead and like me, the song is over 50 years old so I can quote and quote

My mother and father produced gang shows in Essex. When I was seven, a cub scout pulled out of a show, last minute because he was unwell. I learned the lines that morning, dressed up as a termite and took his role in the short comedy sketch. I did well and was asked if

I wanted to join in the finale. All the cast laughed at little Scotty whose erection under his tight white shorts couldn't be hidden. We merrily sang

"We're riding along on a breast of a slave and the tit is in my eye"

I can't remember the next line so I Googled it and 'BDSM big tit teen bdsm bondage slave femdom domination' website (among others) came up. I searched no longer with the realisation of how much life has changed since I was 7

Next year I'll be booked on that cruise again

And the next year, and the next year

It is cheaper than a nursing home

And the food

And the food……

Is to die for

Meditating MS Away

When I told my mother I'd just been diagnosed with
MS she thought I'd got a job at M&S

Reverse it
Reverse it
Reverse it
Reverse it

S&M
S&M
S&M

Bikram yoga
Mirrors and Pillars
Pillars and Mirrors

Bikini clad
Not a fad
3 times a week
Not so weak

(49% of children who have been abused get cancer in
adulthood – there is no research for those who get MS)

Flight into illness
Flight into health
Drink, sex
And the balancing T yoga position
"What does the T stand for ?" asks Cintra our teacher
A chorus of yogis scream "TORTURE"

Mail received at no 6 Elizabeth Avenue, 8th May 1978

Dear Mum and Dad,

I arrived safely in Lloret de Mar. The plane was good but Claire's and my seats had been double booked so the two other people had to get off the plane which delayed us.

We have just been down the town. The things are nice but expensive! We are going to the hotel's disco tonight.

Love Liz

P.S. Make sure dad feeds the fish and finishes the jig-saw!

Dear Liz,

I hope you still love me becuse I still love u. now the football season is nearly over I will be coming down regular starting from sunday, After Spurs have played southampton that is. My mate wants to know how old your sister & friend is? I hope you don't mind but I have scratched Liz on my arm don't worry it didn't hurt we nearly got nicked down brighton when Spurs lost 31 we didn't have a ticket so we had to bunk in. Gary's mate Brian got nicked for kicking a copper in the balls

I still got a bump on my head from were that Spanish bloke hit me over the head with a metal chain. Mind you lucky I was drunk then. Me and Gary are thinking of going away on holiday together. We don't no were yet. Gary wants a photo of your sister and I want a photo of you.

ill see you soon then

Love Tony

Seen but not heard

We sat in the car watching the women outside the flower shop and the tanning shop

We were laughing at them because they looked so orange

We felt protected by the car and its thick glass and the space that separated us

We could have been laughing at something we'd heard on the radio

Or a joke we'd been intimately sharing

We got out of the car and crossed the road

One of the women threw her cigarette lighter at us

It missed and ricocheted off a lamp post on the other side of the road

It was a powerful throw and could have blinded me

If I had been walking backwards

Scene but not herd

"Moo" said the solitary cow
"What's your intention?" said the drama student with intentions to direct

Impatience

I met my 101th boyfriend 4 days after my 100th because my hairdresser told me that the reason I hadn't found the right man was because I didn't give it long enough in between each relationship

Kevin Robertson is back in jail

Kevin oh Kevin oh Kevin oh Kevin,
Another carpenter boyfriend, I expected to already be in heaven
The first time was back in 1987
The post office clerk looked up at him from behind the glass
He said "times must be hard, take off that mask"
Then he pushed the button and Kevin ran
To get into the van
But his mate had already driven off
It was Kevin that would get told off

Two and a half years
Getting off the gear
In Brixton, Saughton, Durham, then
Wandsworth and HMP Send

After detox and relapse
Again and again
This time I left him
To deal with his pain

I had a lucky escape
In 2014 it was too late
For an ex- lover of his
Who is left in the abyss
Of death
Forfar Sheriff Court. D.C Thomson sentenced Kevin
Times had got harder

Keys in Cars in Drives

If I was a car thief I would only work on frosty mornings
And go to residential family areas where there are no garages

With all my other car thief friends we would do the whole street and be done with it

Defrosting the Car

If I was a burglar I would only work on frosty mornings

And go to residential family areas where doors have been left ajar whilst defrosting the car

With all my other burglar friends we would do the whole street and be done with it

He asked to see my minge

Minge isn't a word that I would use, but it comes from real life dialogue from a real person in my real life dream

It was one of those dreams that when you woke up you thought fuck, yes, that could have been real life and it feels like real life, like when I was a child and used to dream about monkeys in the zoo who would put their hands (yes hands, not paws, we are descended from monkeys) through the bars and pull my nose so hard that it really hurt and I would wake up with a throbbing nose

Ricky Gervais was on the phone and he said he wanted to see my minge
"You'll be on set anyway" he said
In real life (outside of the dream) it was a while since I'd done TV extra work and in the dream, I hadn't thought I was working that day so I was a little confused

Nevertheless, having accepted the fact that showing my minge to Ricky was the right thing to do, I began to look for my Motability Vauxhall Zafira, 1.8 with air conditioning, power steering, complete with blue badge for parking and exemption from the congestion charge etc.to get me to Pinewood studios, Buckinghamshire, kind of West London.

I needed to get on set and was getting a feeling of urgency

I thought I'd parked it in the road nearest the flat, but it wasn't there so I went round my dwarf friends who live in a caravan. They have recently got married

I then thought fuck the car, I can't find it. I'll have to go by freedom pass, Uxbridge is the nearest station to Pinewood, not sure if it's in Zone 6, but with a freedom pass you can be very mad and not pay anyway

So then I woke up and wondered about any previous relationship I'd had with Ricky. I only watch reality programmes and Soap operas and I only watch soap operas so I can watch my extra friends and I have never seen the Office, but I did watch Ricky on one episode of Extras so I could see my extra friends being extra extras on Extras

www.ingramcontent.com/pod-product-compliance
Lightning Source LLC
Chambersburg PA
CBHW020959090426
42736CB00010B/1382